# THE BRITISH SOLDIER IN THE 20TH CENTURY

Written and illustrated by

## MIKE CHAPPELL

WESSEX MILITARY PUBLISHING

Published in 1987 by
Wessex Military Publishing
1A High Street
Hatherleigh, Devon EX20 3JH
© Copyright 1987 Wessex
Military Publishing

ISBN 1 870498 01 1

Typeset and printed in Great Britain by
Toptown Printers Limited
Vicarage Lawn, Barnstaple, North Devon
England

*Front Cover:* **The "Brodie" steel helmet of the
Great War period worn with sacking cover (left).
The "soft cap" of 1917 with regimental badge
and flash of the Scots Guards (centre top). A
"Brodie" helmet with the insignia of the pioneer
battalion of the 56th (London) Division (Territorial Force) 1918; the 1/5th Cheshires (centre
below). Lance-Corporal, 10th Battalion the
Parachute Regiment, T.A., 1982.**

*Back Cover:* **Second Lieutenant of the Parachute
Regiment with his signaller, 1986. Note their
current pattern helmets, DPM covers and
"garnish". (MOD HQ UKLF)**

*Right:* **Coldstream Guards private 1918. Note the
way his S.D. cap has been "set up", a fashion
developed to extremes in recent years. (IWM Q
30211)**

# 2 : Field Service Head Dress 1902 to the present day

*"I never saw so many shocking bad hats in my life!" (attributed to the Duke of Wellington)*

In the year 1902 the British Army issued regulations for a "universal" uniform for field service (see volume 1 of this work: Service Dress 1902-1940). With this uniform officers were ordered to wear a cap of the same drab colour with a stiffened, circular crown and a peak set at an angle of sixty degrees.

It took until 1905 for the authorities to decide that a similar cap should be worn by the other ranks of the army. In the meantime, they had been ordered to wear a variety of headgear with Service Dress, including full dress helmets, dark blue Field Service caps, the Brodrick cap of 1903-1905 (sometimes with a drab cover), felt hats, and even the peaked forage cap intended for wear with full dress. All may be seen in photographs of the time and add to the motley appearance of the British soldier at a time when a variety of patterns of equipment, gaiters, leggings, etc were being replaced.

Uniformity had been restored by the time of the outbreak of the Great War. At home the British soldier wore the S.D. cap (sometimes with a waterproof cover), and in tropical climates overseas the "Wolseley" pattern foreign service helmet. The only exception to the rule was the case of the Scottish regiments, who – at home – continued to wear traditional headgear with Service Dress.

From this point in time it is best to study the development of field service head dress item by item.

## The Service Dress Cap

(Called "S.D. cap", "Gor'blimey", "Trench cap", "Soft cap", "Cheese-cutter", etc.")

The battles of 1914 and the winter that followed showed the original S.D. cap to be quite unsuited for campaigning. A trench cap was quickly designed with patterns for officers and other ranks. Both were without crown wires and stiff peaks, and both had a curtain that could be let down to protect the neck and ears. Whilst the officer's trench cap preserved a military appearance, the other rank's pattern

Private, 1/5th Somerset Light Infantry, 75th Division, Palestine, 1918. Note the Wolseley-pattern "topee" and regimental flash. (Collection R.G. Harris)

resembled a civilian cloth cap and was christened "Gor'blimey" – presumably by the first Sergeant-Major to set eyes on one – nevertheless, it was practical and comfortable.

The introduction of steel helmets in 1916 made the trench cap redundant, and in 1917 a soft cap that could be easily packed away began to be issued to other ranks. Officers continued to wear their trench caps as well as S.D. caps with the wires removed.

Between the World Wars there was a return to S.D. caps with wired crowns and stiff peaks, but of a pattern with larger, flatter peaks and with crowns "set up" at the front. The issue of Battledress in 1939/40 restricted the wearing of S.D. caps to a small part of the army which included the Guards, Military Police, animal transport units, bands, boys units, etc.

Officers retained Service Dress on the introduction of Battledress and

Recruits of the 11th (Reserve) Battalion of the Devonshire Regiment pose for their photo at Wareham, Dorset in June 1916. Note the first-pattern S.D. caps worn as issued.

were permitted to wear their S.D. caps with Battledress on certain occasions; many officers wore them on active service.

The S.D. cap is still issued to troops on mounted duties and is worn by most officers as part of "barrack dress". It has survived in service for 85 years and may well continue to be worn in the 21st Century.

## The Field Service Cap

(Called "F.S. cap", "Sidecap", "Fore-and-aft", and a number of unprintable names.)

This extraordinarily impracticable item also survives in service. Issued throughout the army at the turn of the century it was intended to be worn with its peak and neck-and-ear curtain down in inclement weather. At this time the F.S. cap was made up quite plainly and in – mostly – dark blue cloth. Khaki and drab F.S. caps were taken into use in the South African War (by Lord Roberts in particular) and were also issued in the 1914-18 conflict, in which they were the exclusive headgear of the Royal Flying Corps. Regular Army veterans of the 1930's remember the F.S. cap as an issue item for wear with "canvas" – fatigue dress.

Thus the F.S. cap was available at the time of the issue of Battledress and became the cap ordered to be worn with the new uniform, although it gave little protection, frequently fell off – or was blown off – the head, worn (as it was by most soldiers) perched on the side of the head. The cap chosen to replace the F.S. cap in 1943 was seen to be such an abomination that officers and men continued to wear the F.S. cap, when permitted, long after it ceased to be an official item of uniform.

F.S. caps in regimental colours appeared in the years between the World Wars. They were worn extensively with Battledress in barracks, and occasionally in the field. In recent years this "regimental sidecap" has again found popularity in the British Army and is worn as part of barrack dress.

## The General Service Cap

(Called "G.S. cap", "Tammy", "Caps, ridiculous", etc.)

The F.S. cap needed a great deal of material and time to manufacture. It was replaced in 1943 with a cap which was a cross between a Scottish Tam-o-Shanter and a beret, the G.S. cap; an item universally unpopular with those ordered to wear it.

The G.S. cap provided little in the way of protection and, like the beret, could be fashioned into an extraordinary variety of shapes. Some units ordered them to be worn with wire stiffeners, to obtain uniformity, but this made the appearance of the G.S. cap even more ridiculous than usual. The "G.S." remained an item of uniform until the general issue of berets in 1950, and resembled the equally unpopular Brodrick cap of 1903, which was said to make the wearers, "look like a lot of bloody German sailors!".

## The Beret

(Pronounced "Berry" by Tommy.)

The first wearers of berets were the Royal Tank Corps who adopted the item in the 1920s. However, similar headgear – i.e. knitted wool caps with bands and tapes – had been worn previously as Kilmarnock, Glengarry and Balmoral bonnets.

World War Two saw the gradual adoption of the beret in a variety of colours, a practice that continued until practically the entire British Army adopted this particular headgear in 1950. Since that time the only modifications have been to make the beret less voluminous and to replace

(Top) Officers of the Newfoundland Regiment, 29th Division, on the Western Front in 1917 display both the standard S.D. and the "trench" cap. (IWM Q 5336). (Below) Corporal W. Beesley and Sergeant W. Gregg, DCM, MM, at their investiture with the Victoria Cross, France, August 1918. Both wear the "soft cap", instantly recognisable by the stitching on the peak and band. (IWM Q 11134)

the leather band with one made of ribbon. The popularity of the beret is hard to explain. It soaks up rain like a sponge, provides no shade for the eyes, gives hardly any protection from cold weather, cannot be cleaned easily, whilst the colours of the berets worn by most regiments today defy camouflage. (These include scarlet – RMP; cypress green – Intelligence Corps; maroon – Parachute Regiment; light blue – A.A.C.; black and dark blue.)

## The Felt Hat

(Called "Bush hat", "Slouch hat", "Wideawake", "Smasher", "Gurkha hat", etc.)

Felt hats, of one sort or another, have been worn in the British Army for over 300 years. In 1902 consideration was given to the adoption of a felt hat for wear with Service Dress. Felt hats were worn in South Africa 1899-1902 and by units at home up until 1905. Their utility was then well appreciated, they kept the eyes shielded from sun, the rain off the neck, could be used as a container for water and forage, a shield and bellows for firelighting and cover for a pipe or cigarette at night. They appear from photographs to have then conformed to no particular pattern, being worn with the brim pinned up at the right or left

side or left down, with puggarees (long lengths of muslin wound around a hat or helmet, originally wet to cool the head by evaporation) or leather hat bands, chinstraps or not, and of a wide range of drab colours as well as sporting some odd insignia.

Felt hats were once again supplied to the troops in Salonika in 1916, and were worn there and in other stations and theatres in the Middle East. (Some hats originated from charitable "comfort" funds at home. They are recorded as being grey/green on issue, fading to pale pink in the sun.)

In 1942 felt hats began to be issued in large numbers to troops in the Far East, where they continued to be worn until the late 1940's. Once more there were several patterns, usually khaki/drab and usually worn with a khaki drill puggaree. They were nearly always pinned up on the left (to avoid being knocked off when sloping arms) and the crowns were creased in whatever fashion the wearer fancied or authority permitted. (The "pork pie" was popular 1942-45.)

Today the felt hat is worn only by men of the Brigade of Gurkhas.

## The Sun Helmet

(Called "Overseas helmets", "Wolseley helmets", "Pith hats/helmets",

(Top) The "Brodie" helmet being worn at the battle of the Somme, 1st July 1916. (IWM Q 65414). (Below) Tank crew visor as at (h) opposite. (IWM Q 14599)

(continued on page 18)

HELMETS 1915-1944. The standard steel helmet of the Great War was the MARK I or "BRODIE", shown in profile at (a) with the black-and-yellow marking of 'Z' Company, 2nd Hampshires, 1918. The front view at (b) has the device of the 9th Royal Fusiliers, 1917. Note the "dished" brim. The Mark I had two different patterns of liner/chinstrap. Both were secured by a copper rivet, and – as the rivet frequently sheared with wear – the liners were sometimes worn as caps. (First pattern (c); second pattern (d)). Viewed in plan the Mark I helmet was circular in shape, contrasting with the MARK II shown at (e) with Royal Artillery markings. The Mark II was introduced just prior to the Second World War; it had a chinstrap made of webbing and steel springs and the brim was flat. At (f) the Mark II helmet is shown in the red markings of the Military Police. In 1944 a MARK III helmet with an elasticated webbing chinstrap began to be issued (shown at (g) with Coldstream Guards markings). TANK CREWS were issued with a rivetted fibre helmet in 1916. This was worn with goggles and face mask as at (h). Later in the Great War tank crews wore the Mark I "Brodie" helmet with chain mail "CRUISE" visors; the second pattern of which is shown at (j). In World War Two there was a reversion to fibre helmets for Tank crews, with several patterns all conforming to the basic configuration shown at (k). (Marking for 2nd Grenadiers, Guards Armoured Division, 1942.)

**The Service Dress Cap.**

*(a) Private soldier of the 16th Bn the London Regiment, Queen's Westminster Rifles, Territorial Force 1914. The standard other rank's cap of the time, worn by this unit with insignia similar to the regular King's Royal Rifle Corps, an officer of which is depicted at (b) with the officer's pattern trench cap in 1915. Trench caps featured a protective flap, which when lowered gave rise to the appellation "Gor'blimey". The other rank's Gor'blimey is shown at (c), with the battle patch adopted by the 1/8th Sherwood Foresters in 1915. At (d) is an officer's cap of the Duke of Cornwall's Light Infantry, with a waterproof cover. Chinstraps on O.R.'s caps had brass "furniture", whilst those on officer's caps had leather "sliders".*

*A portrait of General Sir Harold Alexander in 1944 is shown at (e), demonstrating the cap of a General officer of the time. "Staff" caps evolved from the forage caps worn before the Great War. These were first worn with drab covers and were later made up with drab crowns and peaks. A junior Staff officer's cap of 1914 is shown at (f) with the appropriate gorget patch beside it. (g) Royal Army Medical Corps Colonel, 1914. (h) Intelligence staff officer, 1916. (j) Staff Colonel, Administration, 1914. (k) Staff officer, Royal Flying Corps, 1917. (1) Staff cap badge.*

*With the introduction of Battledress in 1939/40 the Corps of Military Police continued to wear the Service Dress cap on which they wore a red cap cover when on duty, as demonstrated by (m) Sergeant, Provost company, 13th Infantry Division, Greece 1946. (Military Police units responsible for the protection of vital points wore a blue cap cover (o) in World War Two.) A white cap cover (n) is worn in the Royal Artillery by assistant instructors of Gunnery, here depicted in the 1950's. At this time also other ranks of the Foot Guards continued to wear the S.D. cap with Battledress, but "set up" in the manner shown at (p). The cap worn by their officers is shown at (q) worn by a Scots Guards Major in 1950. Compare this with the Grenadier Guards S.D. cap worn by the Prince of Wales in 1914 (left, below). Compare also the General officers cap worn by General Alexander in World War Two with that worn by Lieutenant-General Maude (left, above) in the Great War. The gold oak leaves on the peaks of the earlier caps gave rise to the name "brass hats", an epithet that almost certainly led to General officers and staff adopting less florid headgear.*

a

b

c

d

e

f

g

h

j

k

l

m

p

n

q

o

r

s

t

u

## COLOUR PLATE B

### Scottish Regiments.

*With the adoption of Service Dress the appropriate head dress for Scottish Regiments was deemed to be either the Glengarry, ((a) Black Watch officer; (b) 5th Seaforth Highlanders; (c) Scottish Rifles officer; (d) Royal Scots; (e) Gordon Highlanders officer; and (right above) Argyll and Sutherland Highlanders – all 1914) or some form of flat bonnet ((f) Scottish Horse; (g) Lovat Scouts; and Territorial Bns of the Highland Light Infantry and Argylls – not shown). These were found to be unsuitable for active service in the opening months of the Great War and were replaced by a plain blue Balmoral (j – Argylls) which was either worn with a drab cover (k – Seaforths) or simply turned inside-out to reveal a drab lining. A drab Balmoral began to be issued in 1915, (m – Camerons officer; o – Royal Scots Fusilier) and in the same year a Balmoral-type bonnet fabricated from drab serge material began to be issued. Called the "Tam-o-Shanter" bonnet it survives to this day as the field service head dress of the Scottish Regiments. At first the shape of the T.O.S. was very broad (n – Piper Laidlaw, VC, King's Own Scottish Borderers, 1915). The practice of wearing tartan patches on T.O.S. bonnets began in the 9th (Scottish) Division in 1915. Battalions of the Division were ordered to wear these distinctions in the manner of "battle patches"; cap badges were not to be worn in the line. At (p) is the patch of the 5th Camerons, and at (q) that of the 8th Gordons. These patches almost certainly derived from the old puggaree flashes of former times and were worn with cap badges when out of the line. The fashion started by the 9th Division was gradually copied and survives to this day.*

*Over the years the T.O.S. bonnet has "shrunk" to its present size (r – Royal Highland Fusiliers, 1980's) through the intermediate dimensions of World War Two (s – 10th H.L.I., 15th (Scottish) Infantry Division, 1944 and – right below – 1st Camerons, 2nd Infantry Division, 1945). Comparisons can be made with (n) and (t – Drum Major 7th Black Watch, 51st (Highland) Division, 1917). When first issued the T.O.S. had two drab ribbon "tails" similar to those on the Glengarry and Balmoral. These were sometimes worn as issued, or tied in a bow or knot (u – 1/8th King's, Liverpool Scottish, 55th (W. Lancashire) Division, 1917). Eventually the T.O.S. was manufactured with a false bow. Officers adopted a T.O.S. bonnet of a paler shade of drab in the Great War and this practice has survived to the present day.*

11

Infantry battle order. Left, Germany 198
(disruptive pattern material) cover and e
HQ UKLF). Right, India 1915. A bugler o
Wolseley-pattern helmet, or topee. Note t
(Collection D. Quarmby)

Above. A selection of less well-known fie
drill cover, 1904; (b) the cap, comforter – u
by a similar item, the "headover", recentl
fur cap worn in Russia and the Far East l
1940-1950's, Combat dress 1950-1970's, D

d

e

general service combat helmet, its DPM
web "garnish" straps clearly visible (MOD
Hampshires protected from the sun by his
n puggaree flash (see also colour plate Cj).

headgear. (a) the Brodrick cap with khaki
e early years of the century until replaced
lava helmets, used in both World Wars; (d)
(e) Combat caps (top to bottom) ski troops

**Tropical Head Dress.**

*In 1902 the old overseas cork sun helmet (a – West Yorkshire Regt) was in the process of being replaced by the "Wolseley" pattern (b – officer, Northumberland Fusiliers, 1930). The Wolseley helmet was made of cork and covered in khaki drill; officers' helmets had leather brim bindings, other ranks webbing tape. The Wolseley was officially replaced in India by the pith hat (c – 1st Glosters, 1941) in the 1930's, but both patterns were worn from before 1902 until they were deemed no longer necessary during World War Two.*

*Felt hats had been worn by the British at various times since 1660. They were worn in South Africa (d – Scots Guards) during the war of 1899-1902 and at home and overseas afterwards. Felt hats were supplied to the troops in Salonika during the Great War (e – 1st Suffolks, 1916 and photo above left). In 1942 the felt hat began to be issued in large numbers to the troops fighting the Japanese in the Far East (n – Warrant Officer, Royal Corps of Signals, 1945). A hat made of drill cloth was issued to British personnel serving with the Indian Army in 1945 (f – Artillery) and from this developed the jungle hat issued from the late 1940's (g – 'B' Company, 1st Royal Hampshires, 1954, and photo left below).*

*Identification "flashes" stitched to helmet covers and puggarees during the Boer War became a feature on tropical head dress in the 20th Century. At (h) are those for the Lancashire Fusiliers 1899-1902 (cut from tunic shoulder straps); 83rd Field Battery, R.A., 1930's and 1/4th Wiltshires, 1915. At (j) are puggaree flashes worn by the Hampshire Regiment in India during the Great War; 2/4th Battalion, 1/9th (Cyclist) Battalion; and 2/5th Battalion.*

*Neck curtains were worn occasionally for added protection from the sun. (k) a British officer with a Battalion of the Frontier Force Rifles, 1945; (l) 9th Royal Warwicks, 1916; and 2nd Black Watch, 1918.*

*Some fusilier regiments wore miniatures of their busby plumes on tropical head dress. (o) Battalions of the Lancashire Fusiliers, India 1942. (Note that the flash was by now rectangular.) (p) Prior to their disbandment in 1922 the Royal Munster Fusiliers wore a shoulder title pinned through a shamrock patch to secure their plume.*

*(Photographs; collection R.G. Harris and MOD HQ UKLF)*

Plate C

## COLOUR PLATE D

### General Service Caps and Berets

*The limitations of the field service or "side" cap were apparent long before 1943, but it took until this time for a replacement to appear. This was the general service (G.S.) cap, an item of headgear almost as un-popular as the Brodrick cap of forty years before. Wartime economy spawned the G.S. cap and the plastic badges ordered worn in them (a – Royal Electrical and Mechanical Engineers). Patches of coloured cloth were adopted to smarten up the drabness of the G.S. cap and the black, brown or grey plastic badges (b – 6th Durham Light Infantry; d – Northamptonshire Regiment; e – Essex Regiment. All 1944). Irish Regiments wore the G.S. cap in the manner of the traditional Irish "caubeen" bonnet (c – London Irish Rifles, 1944; and photo – above, right – of Colour-Sergeant Sharkey, 2nd Royal Ulster Rifles, receiving the ribbon of the D.C.M. in 1944 from Field-Marshal Montgomery). Not all Irish regiments chose to pull the "caubeen" down to the left.*

*The wearing of berets in the British Army dates from the adoption of the black beret (h) by the Royal Tank Corps in 1924. In 1928 the 11th Hussars adopted a brown beret (q) with a "cherry" band, and in 1941 black berets were authorised for all units of the Royal Armoured Corps. In 1942 Air-borne Forces adopted a maroon beret (j – 7th (Light Infantry) Battalion, the Parachute Regiment, 1944) and shortly afterwards the Commandos adopted the green beret (f – Commando N.C.O., ex-Gordon Highland-ers, 1945. 9 Commando wore a black hackle as at (n).) The Reconnaissance Corps adopted a "khaki" beret in 1943 (k), but as this item was extensively scrounged for wear in place of the G.S. cap the significance waned. A sand-coloured beret was being worn by units of the Special Air Service in 1944 (l). (The SAS are said to have adopted a white beret early in their existence.)*

*In 1950 the G.S. cap was replaced with a dark blue beret (g – N.C.O. Lancashire Fusiliers, 1957. Note the feather hackle and positioning of the badge). Rifle Regiments and Light Infantry were issued with dark green berets (m – King's Shropshire Light Infantry, 1952); Irish Regiments were issued with "caubeens" of the appropriate colour (o – officer, Royal Inniskilling Fusiliers, 1950's). With the creation of the Army Air Corps in the 1950's the beret at (p) was adopted.*

*Probably the most famous black beret was "Monty's" – see photo above, right – always worn with two badges. The photo below right shows the maroon beret worn by Private Kearn of the 1st Border Regiment, 1st Airborne Division, 1944.*

"Cork helmets", etc, but almost always referred to by the troops as "Topees", the Hindustani word for hat.)

Helmets of compressed and moulded cork had been in use for many years by the dawn of the 20th Century. One pattern, usually covered in blue cloth, was for home service, and a similar item covered in white drill was intended for service in tropical climates overseas. On campaign the overseas helmet was worn with a khaki drill cover.

By 1902 the overseas helmet was being replaced by the Wolseley, a better-designed helmet. This was to remain a standard issue until the middle of the Second World War, when army medical authorities declared them redundant. The Wolseley was made in English factories, but in India a sun helmet had been made for many years from wicker and pith covered in khaki drill. Both sun helmets remained on issue from 1902, with the pith hat supplanting the Wolseley for Indian Service from the middle 1930's.

Both helmets were worn with puggarees, which by 1902 had long ceased to have any practical use, becoming items of decoration on which regiments wore their colours or "flashes" in lieu of cap badges.

A tradition of the old Regular Army was that of throwing topees overboard from troopships on sighting England after a long tour abroad. As a boy in September 1939, the author added his topee to the hundreds bobbing upside down in the wake of the trooper approaching the Solent. It was a rare moment.

"Combien chuffler Madame?". Tommy bargaining for vegetables, St. Omer, 1918. Note the "soft cap" of this Royal Field Artilleryman. (IWM)

## The Steel Helmet

(Called "Tin hat", "Battle bowler", "Tin topee", etc.)

In late 1915 the British were forced to follow the example of their allies and their enemies and order what were termed "shrapnel" helmets for their troops on the Western Front. Officers had been able to buy steel helmets (as well as body armour) from their outfitters prior to this, but issues of the first regulation helmet – later called the "Brodie" after its designer – only began in the winter of 1915/16 and took until mid-1916 to complete. With very slight modifications the "Brodie" served until the late 1930's, when a similar helmet offering more ballistic protection replaced it. By now these helmets had acquired the titles of Mark I and Mark II.

In 1944 a Mark III helmet of considerably different shape began to be issued, and this had replaced the Mark II by the early 1950's. The Mark III was modified in succeeding Marks with improved liners and riot visors until it was replaced recently by a plastic general service combat helmet – an item developed after much research and practical experience with plastic helmets in Northern Ireland.

Camouflaging helmets has always been a problem. In the Great War fabric covers were much used by the British, who reverted to them briefly in 1939/40 before adopting netting as the best medium for holding camouflage material – referred to as "garnish" in the British Army. Lately there has been a reversion to fabric covers — in Disruptive Pattern Material (DPM).

## Other Forms of Headgear

So far, what might be termed as "mainstream" items of field service head dress have been examined. Less well-known items are described in this chapter.

Knitted wool caps and helmets have always been worn in the field and include the "Cap, comforter" worn for patrolling and Commando operations; the Balaclava helmet of both World Wars; The woollen toque or "head-over" issued today; and the knitted steel helmet liner of recent years.

Sniping required special attention to camouflage. In the Great War snipers' hoods were made from hessian, or sacking, and daubed with paint or mud. In World War Two much use was made of the netting face veil.

Goggles, face shields and masks have been in use since the Great War, both issued and improvised items, providing protection from the elements, bullet splash and projectile backblast.

Exceptionally cold weather has seen the issue of fur or pile caps, from Russia in 1918, through Korea in the 1950's to the Falklands in recent years.

*(continued on page 24)*

HELMETS 1940 – present day. The Mark II steel helmet proved to be of little use to the fledgling British parachute troops in 1940. Their first effective protective headgear was the helmet at (a) made from crudely moulded sorbo rubber. This material was also used in the later canvas helmet at (b). The first steel helmet for airborne troops appeared in 1941/42 and had a hard rubber brim and a leather head-harness (c). A second-pattern rubber brim (d) soon replaced the first. (Note detail of chinstrap buckle.) In the final-pattern airborne helmet the brim was discarded, and later a webbing head-harness replaced the leather pattern. The steel shell of the third-pattern airborne helmet was used with the liner and chinstrap of the Mark III steel helmet to produced the Royal Armoured Corps steel helmet in 1943. The shell was also used to produce the despatch rider's Mk I steel helmet (f) at about the same time. (A composition helmet had been worn by motor cyclists until this time. Note the tactical number for a machine gun battalion.) Trials with plastic helmets in the 1970's and 1980's have resulted in the recent introduction of the parachutist's lightweight helmet at (g), the general service combat helmet at (h) and the armoured fighting vehicle crewman's helmet at (j).

The young "Monty" is seen, above left, as a Brigade Major in 1916 wearing the "battle bowler" steel helmet purchased by officers from their outfitters. Compare it with the regulation "Brodie" worn by the General beside Montgomery. Seen in photographs taken in late 1915 and early 1916, the "battle bowler" has not been noted later. Officers' outfitters bought the shells of the "Brodie" helmet from the factories, as they became available, and fitted them with superior quality leather linings.

Top right. Devon gunners of the Wessex Division in India, 1915. Dressed in bazaar-made uniforms, they are ready for "walking out". The "topee" was not worn after sundown. The F.S. cap, here the old dark blue pattern, was the prescribed item.

Left. The Tam-o-Shanter. Worn here by a young private of the 6th King's Own Scottish Borderers, 1918. Note how large an item the original bonnet was. Note also the strips of coloured cloth worn on the shoulders in the 9th (Scottish) Division to indicate the company of the wearer.

Above left. The Mark II steel helmet 1943. Worn by a private of the 6th Gordons, 1st Infantry Division, as he searches a German prisoner-of-war in Tunisia. The Mk II had a distinctive shape and could not be confused with the Mark I "Brodie" of the Great War. As World War Two developed, so the outline of British Army steel helmets disappeared under layers of sacking, nets, hessian "scrim" and foliage "garnish" – all in the furtherance of camouflage. (IWM)

Above right. The officer's pattern S.D. cap worn by Brigadiers of the 46th Infantry Division, N. Africa, 1943. The junior officers of the Great War, on assuming senior rank in the Second World War, avoided "brasshat" costume. Only their cap bands, gorget patches and badges of rank set them apart in Battledress. (IWM)

Right. Private soldier, 2/4th Hampshires, 4th Infantry Division, Italy, 1944. Pte. L. Palmer wears the F.S. cap and a "Lease-lend" U.S. Army O.D. wool shirt.

Above. The jungle hat. Korea, 1952. Men of the 1st K.O.S.B. at a mortar position. Note the patches of regimental tartan.

Below. The blue beret. N.C.O's "cadre", Wessex Brigade Depot, Exeter, 1956. Note the insignia of the Devons, Glosters, Royal Hampshires and the Royal Berkshires. (Author on the left of Sgt. Thomas.)

Above. The Airborne Forces steel helmet, 1980's. Just prior to its replacement by the present plastic helmet and well "camouflaged up". (MOD HQ UKLF)

Below. The Mark IV steel helmet underwent several modifications to its liner before being replaced by a plastic helmet. Here, in the 1980's an 84-mm Anti-Tank gun team wear steel helmets "garnished" with sacking and plastic "scrim". (MOD HQ UKLF)

Combat or ski caps – with long peaks and earflaps – were first issued in the British Army in 1940, since when there have been three patterns. Surprisingly, these practical items have never been popular, with the beret, T.O.S. or caubeen being worn for preference.

Another form of protective headgear are the various anti-gas helmets, masks and respirators worn since 1915. These will be covered in later titles dealing with equipment.

Hoods have been designed into tank suits, ponchos, parkas and combat clothing over the last forty years or so. They may therefore be mentioned as headgear by virtue of their protective function. They also restrict vision and hearing, and so have limited use.

Flying helmets are considered outside the scope of this book.

## Head Dress Insignia

The British soldier is generally proud of the Regiment or Corps in which he serves. Issue him with a cap, helmet or hat and he will fix or paint his cap badge on it unless ordered not to do so. The amazing variety of cap badges, puggaree flashes, battle patches, plumes, feathers and hackles worn this century is a study in itself. Those illustrated in this book have been included to show what was typical, or unusual, or as an indication as to how they were worn. Whilst attempting to show an example of all the items of head dress worn in the field since 1902, the reader should appreciate that the insignia illustrated represents a minute part of the total worn since that time.

**The driver of an A.F.V. in Norway, 1980's. He wears the D.P.M. pile cap, snow goggles and intercommunication headset. (MOD HQ UKLF)**

24